TABLE OF CONTENTS

Your Mouth Confessing God's Healing Promises Will Heal Your Disease

I Was Healed of Multiple Myeloma, an Incurable Blood Disease!

Ronald P. Braddock, Sr.

INTRODUCTION

In February 2019, I was diagnosed with cancer of the blood known as multiple myeloma. This is an incurable disease, and the goals of treatment are to stop the progressive state of this disease and put it in remission. Well, I started treatments right away that were six thirty-day cycles to try to stop its advancement.

I am retired now. But years ago, when I was marketing manager of Georgia and Tennessee for my company, I was traveling many hours in my car covering these two states. I had a strong desire to know the New Testament, so I bought CDs of the New Testament to listen to while I was traveling. Over the years I must have listened to them more or less seventy times, so I was very knowledgeable of the Bible.

The Lord knew that I knew what to do and how to do it. I go into much detail in this book, but briefly I looked up healing promises of the Bible and confess these promises over and over daily.

In only two months and two weeks in the third cycle, my doctor said that I had made remarkable improvement.

After getting the good news so quickly, my wife and I decided to get a second opinion from Emory Hospital from a specialist who only dealt with this disease. We made an appointment and sent all my files to him to examine. In addition, they did their own blood test. Hours later that day, we met with the specialist, and briefly this was his evaluation: everything looks great. He also made a point to tell me that when he examined a blood test report, there were two very important items that he looked at—the lower the number of these items, the better. He said, "One item when you were first diagnosed was 2,000; now it is 200, an 1,800 drop. The other item was 200 at the start, and now it is a 16, an incredible turnaround." After several months, I asked my regular cancer doctor this question: do I have any bad cancer cells in my body according to my blood test? He said, "Not a trace."

One day I was praying and giving thanks to the Lord and said, "Wouldn't it be great if all my brothers and sisters in Christ knew how to do this and be healed?"

The Lord said, "Why don't you tell them?"

So I'm writing my second book for you and the glory of the Lord.

*I Was Healed of Multiple Myeloma,
an Incurable Blood Disease!*

Your Mouth Confessing
God's Healing Promises
Will Heal Your Disease

RONALD P. BRADDOCK, SR.

ARPress
ILLUMINATING IDEAS
EMPOWERING VOICES

ARPress
45 Dan Road Suite 5
Canton MA 02021
Hotline: 1(888) 821-0229
Fax: 1(508) 545-7580

Ordering Information:
Quantity sales. Special discounts are available on quantity purchases by corporations, associations, and others. For details, contact the publisher at the address above.

Printed in the United States of America.

ISBN-13:   Softcover   979-8-89356-730-4
                 eBook   979-8-89356-731-1

Library of Congress Control Number: 2024906119

GENERAL INFORMATION

The main topic of this book is "how to use God's promises to heal your body when cancer or any other disease comes to you."

Would you know *what* to do and *how* to do it? Probably not. Okay, you would know to pray. However, when cancer or any other serious disease comes, fear comes with it.

So, if you pray for healing in fear, that prayer will not get out of the room you are praying in.

The reason you would not know "what" and "how" is because you have never been taught these things. This is why I am writing this book, to teach you what to do and how to do it. Everything that I am going to teach you, I have already done it. I had cancer.

Before I go any further, I am "not" saying don't go to the doctor. As a matter of fact, I am saying for you to go to your doctor and go through any treatments your doctor recommends. But you need to do both. Do the treatments, and do the teaching in this book.

If the doctor told you that you have a fatal disease, those words he spoke could take your hope of living away.

God's promises can give you your hope back. God's promises are saying, "You can live and not die."

Bless the Lord o my soul and forget not all His *benefits*: who forgives all our sins and heals *all* our diseases. (Psalm 103:2–3, emphasis mine)

Would this scripture give you your hope back? I would think so! This is King David talking about Jesus. All Jesus needs is for you to implement your faith with this promise to receive your healing. I am going to teach you what the Bible says about how to do this.

You might say or think that you don't know if you got the faith to believe. Yes, you do! You believed Jesus died on the cross for your sins, didn't you? You can believe because I'm going to help you. Jesus is willing to heal you. Are you willing to accept his power? Believing or not believing is a decision that only you can make, so decide to believe and be healed!

I realize that what I said probably shocked you because we have put all our confidence in our medical doctors. I know our medical professionals have been able to do great things with the sickness and diseases that are present in our lives. But have we (believers) forgotten the greatest Healer of all time: the Word of God, Jesus Christ?

Did you know that there are many healing scriptures in the Bible? Why did God put these healing promises in the Bible if not for us to use them?

Our faith in God's Word concerning Jesus Christ's cross was our salvation. Is it so hard to believe that God's healing promises can heal your body of any sickness or disease that may come on your body? Have we drifted away from our benefits of healing from God? I am *not* saying for you to pick one of the two, healing promises or the doctors. I am saying to pick both.

My number one objective for writing this book is to teach you what to do and how to do it—God's way!

God's Word made everything that was made, and there is nothing made that wasn't made by him, Jesus Christ (John 1.3).

1. God's Word can save your soul.
2. God's Word can heal your body.
3. God's Word can supply all your needs.
4. God's Word can give you your desires.
5. God's Word can give you an abundant life.

God's Word is the "source." All he needs is for you to believe. God's Word is the most powerful power that there is. And he has given us his Word (healing promises) to believe and bring us to whatever we need. God is able, God is willing, and God is ready to heal you. Are you willing? Believe and give glory to God.

CHRISTIANS

Most Christians go to church on Sunday and have accepted Jesus as Lord and Savior. They love the Lord and are going to heaven when they die. However, that does not mean that you have a lot of knowledge of the New Testament, the gospel of Jesus Christ.

As a matter of fact, you probably know very little. That's okay because after reading my two books, that is going to change greatly.

My first book is titled *Every Christian Should Read This Book*. This book tells you

1. Adam and Eve's sin in the garden of Eden,

2. The effect that Adam's sin had on the human race, and

3. Why God had to send Jesus into the world to be crucified for man's sin and raised from the dead so that we could be raised from the dead unto life. We got born again and forgiven of our sins. Both were important, and salvation was complete.

My first book tells us how God sees us, now that we have been forgiven of all sin and raised from the dead unto life.

I know you will enjoy it and your knowledge will be increased greatly. Now, let's get back to you (Christians).

You must believe God's healing promises in order to be healed of your disease. If you are doing things that you know are wrong, whatever they may be, your conscience will condemn you and hinder your faith.

So I suggest that you write this down on a piece of paper and go into your prayer room and start your prayer with "Father, I come to you in the name of Jesus" and confess these wrongs that you have done and receive your forgiveness. The Word says that if we confess our sins, God will forgive us and cleanse us from all unrighteousness. So turn away from these wrongs and thank God for his forgiveness, and then forgive yourself for what you have done. Be sincere with God. Don't listen to the devil and what he is telling you, because he is a liar! Confess and move on; confess out loud so you can hear yourself.

When God forgives you, he cleanses your conscience, and now your faith is not hindered. Very important scripture here:

Holding the mystery of the faith in a pure [clean] conscience. (1 Timothy 3:9)

Always have a clean conscience, and confession is the way to have it. Don't forget that you are under the grace of God for your wrongdoing—but wrongdoing will affect the strength of your faith and your power. (God did not give you a spirit of fear but of power, love, and a sound mind [2 Timothy 1:7].)

Now, you have a clean conscience and are in position with no hindrance to your faith to believe God's promises for your healing. Sounds too easy? It is easy and simple. God wanted it that way, because he wants to heal you in times of need. You belong to him. You are his children. God did not bring sickness and disease in the world—sin did and if sin then the devil himself. The Lord is your protection.

Now, let's talk about another obstacle, *fear*. Fear also came from the devil. When you are in fear, there is no faith. When you are in faith, there is no fear. The Bible says over and over again to "fear not," and what do we do? We fear things that have not happened because Satan has told our minds, "What if this happens? What if… What if…" And you listen to this because you don't know that it is him (devil). He has put these what-ifs in your head. You think that it is you who is thinking these what-ifs? It is him! It's time that you start recognizing that you will hear two voices in your head. One is the Holy Spirit, and the other is the devil or one of his fallen angels.

But know this: when any Christian is believing God's Word for something, the fallen angels of Satan are going to try to get you to doubt— don't be surprised, but be prepared. Call him out and say, "I resist you, you evil spirit, and I am committed to God. I resist you in the name of Jesus." Then praise God and move on.

When you call him out, he knows that you know he is there and he lost his cover. This is the spiritual world that we live in now, and it is not going to change until we die and go to heaven. "The just shall live by faith" (in the Word of God) (Hebrews 10:38).

The devil has convinced us that fear is a natural emotion. That is a lie. Fear came in the world when sin came in the world. The Bible says, "Fear not." So Christians *must* make a decision to not fear. Fear will hinder your thinking and destroy your faith.

I do understand that if you got diagnosed with a serious or fatal disease, it would shake you. When the doctor told me of my cancer, I was in a state of shock for three days. After I got over the shock, I said, "What now?" Take some time to get over the bad news. When you are thinking clearly, get busy on the teaching of this book.

I always said only God can make something good out of something bad.

If I had not gone through what you will be going through, I would not be writing this book on healing. I have no doubt that what I am telling you will heal you of your disease. God is involved in this. I did not volunteer to write this book until he asked me. Then I said, "Okay, Lord. Yes, I will for you and my brothers and sisters in your name."

Going back, I always wondered, *Why am I doing this? Listening and listening and reading and meditating on the Word of God for what? Myself? No!*

God was preparing me for this, and I did not know it until now.

One last thought. You have accepted Jesus Christ for the forgiveness of your sins. You have been born again; you are a new creation. God has not given you a new spirit of fear but of power and love and a sound mind. Everyone is capable of making a decision, and that is what you have to do. You have to make a decision to believe God's Word to be healed. And you must believe this way. *You must believe that you have received your healing before there is any physical evidence.* Your faith (believing) will bring the healing to your body with patience. It is like what Jesus said. It is like when man cast seed (the Word of God) in the ground (your spirit) and slept night and day and the seed (Word of God) sprung and grew up and he knew not how. When it grows up, that is the manifestation on the physical appearance of your healing (Mark 4:26–27).

Suggestion: While you are waiting on the healing to appear, praise God every day for your healing, thanking him! This is spiritual and how to receive God's supernatural power. Believe first. Then receive.

THE AUTHOR

Who am I? Do you know who you are? You are more than a name. I am a son of the Almighty God, and I go by the name of Ronald P. Braddock Sr. on this earth. This is whom I became when I received Jesus Christ as my Lord and Savior; and that is who you are, a son or daughter of the Most High God.

When I was in my mid-forties, my wife and I and our two kids were at church every Sunday. The pastor preached about salvation with a church full of saved people. I learned of course that we are children of God. But I knew that I really did not know this God in heaven who is my Heavenly Father.

So I asked a pastor, "How does one get to know our so-called Father in heaven?"

He said, "Read the New Testament, and God will reveal himself to you in his Word."

I started to read the New Testament, and the strangest thing kept on happening.

I would fall asleep before I could read one page. This kept on happening over and over again. So one day, before I started to read, I prayed this prayer:

"Lord, every time I start to read your Word to get to know you and my Heavenly Father better, I fall asleep. How can you help me?"

After that prayer, I started to read, and I fell asleep. I woke up, and I got up off the sofa and looked down and saw myself sound asleep. I turned and looked toward the kitchen and saw a man standing there. He was wearing a white robe, and somehow, I knew it was Jesus.

I walked into the kitchen and said to him the same thing that I prayed about. He (Jesus) said to me, "Go over to the table and drink the water in the pitcher."

So I went over, picked up the pitcher of water, and began to drink. However, I could hardly drink but a few swallows. I turned back to him and said, "I can't drink the water."

Jesus then said, "Go now to the entrance of the subdivision and come back." I went out the front door and started running at a great speed. I came back and went back to the kitchen, and he said, "Now go drink the water."

I went over to the table, picked up the pitcher, and drank every drop. I turned back to him and said, "I don't understand."

Jesus said, "Why could you drink the water the second time and not the first?"

I said, "Because the second time I was thirsty."

He then replied to me, "Ask me for a thirst for my Word, and I will give it to you." So I asked, and he said, "You have it."

He then disappeared, and I woke up from sleeping. I didn't know what to think. Everything seemed so real. I finally came to the conclusion that it had to be a dream. But afterward, my thirst for the Word was incredible.

At this time, I was a marketing manager for Georgia and Tennessee, traveling in my car four to five hours at a time covering those two states. I got the idea to buy some CDs of the New Testament to listen to while I was driving.

The first time I listened to Matthew through Revelation, I cried my eyes out. I had no idea about the love of Christ and God the Father. The second time that I listened to the New Testament, it was different. It was like the Holy Spirit was explaining things to me. It was like a teaching class. The third time it was very much the same. After three times of listening, my life has never been the same. My knowledge and faith increased, and it was exciting to learn so much about the Bible. I never got tired of listening to the same stories over and over again.

The Bible says, "Faith comes from hearing and hearing by the word of God" (Romans 10:17). I kept on listening, and faith kept on coming. I did this for years. I never kept count, but I used to say that I had listened to the New Testament one hundred times. But I didn't want to exaggerate, so I changed that number to seventy-plus times.

My prayer time greatly increased, and I got the feeling that I was so special to the Lord, but later I realized that every child of God is special to him. God is God, and he can make every believer feel like he is the only son he has, when he has millions.

Anyway, my love for Jesus and God the Father is great. My faith in God is great, and my confidence in the Word of God is great.

I am not alone, for all believers love the Lord with all their spirit (heart) and their soul and with all their mind. And, because of your love for the Lord, what I am going to teach you is going to be easy. It is easy to have faith and trust in someone whom you love. This someone is the Lord who has the power to deliver whatever his Word says.

Nevertheless, one (Christian) might say, "Well, I haven't been doing some things that I know I should, and I am doing some things that I know I shouldn't do. Now what?"

One prayer of confessing those wrongs and turning away from them can put you in position to believe God. You confess with a serious heart, and he (God) forgives and cleanses you from all your wrongs. It is time for all Christians to rethink about how they are living and give up anything that is unpleasing to God.

After hearing the New Testament about ten-plus times while I was traveling, I was in my prayer room, and I said to the Lord, "I will do anything that you ask of me. No matter what it is, I will do it." I really did not think that he, the Lord, would ever ask me to do anything. I was wrong.

My wife would go to a Christian gathering with people from the church about once every two weeks. They had one, and during the meeting, a lady came into the room and told them that she had been diagnosed with some form of cancer that was very aggressive and life-threatening. Her name was Anne Minsor. I really did not recognize the name of whom she was talking about.

When she finished telling me the story, I asked her, "What did you and the ladies do?"

She said, "Nothing. We were all in a state of shock."

Here's what came out of my mouth: "Why didn't all of you put her in a chair and pray over her and lay hands on her and God would have healed her?"

I was shocked that I said that, but I was filled with faith, and the Word says out of the abundance of the heart the mouth will speak. I went back to having my coffee, and the spirit that dwells in all Christians spoke to me, "I want you to go pray for that lady." So I went into my room, took my shoes off (I always do that), and prayed for her. My prayer went something like this: I told the Lord she was only thirty-five years young, a Christian lady with a husband and two children who loved him, and she was too young to die. I prayed earnestly for the Lord to heal her.

After I finished praying, I was sitting on the floor crying, and I heard the spirit say, "I am going to heal her." His voice was a surprise, but I was glad to hear what he said.

I said, "That's great."

Then he said, "I am going to heal her through you."

Then I said, "What do you mean you are going to heal her through me?"

He said, "Call her on the phone and tell her that your wife gave you the information about the cancer this morning and you got the urge to pray for her healing and the spirit of God told you that he is going to heal her and he is going to do it through you. Tell her exactly that!" I turned white as a sheep. I was so shocked at what he told me, and he knew it. I had never done anything like this in my life. Then he said, "Did you say that you would do anything that I ask you to do? Well, I am asking you do this."

Well, my nerves were shaken, but I got enough courage to make the call. On the phone, I told her exactly how all this transpired. She replied, "When are you coming?" We agreed on 11:00 a.m. that day. I went over to her house and got out of my car, and she was waiting in the driveway. We hugged and went into the house.

I told her again how all this happened, and she asked a few questions, and then I said to her, "Are you ready to receive your healing?"

She replied, "Yes, I am."

I put my hands on her head and prayed, and the last words I spoke were "In the name of Jesus Christ, you are healed."

One month and two weeks later, she went back to the doctor, and she was told "The cancer is *gone*."

That was a very dramatic experience for me then, but my faith went sky- high. I have had a lot of great things happen after that, but that one was the best to share with you at this time.

Now years have gone by, and my relationship with the Lord has remained strong. In 2019, I was praying in my prayer room, and I was thanking God for all the things he had done for me. I told the Lord that I would like to do something for him, having no idea what that might be.

I have studied the Bible for years, but the apostle Paul's revelation of the cross of Jesus Christ was complicated for me. For your information, there is more to the cross of Jesus than the forgiveness of sins, although that is one of the biggest things that happened. The other big thing was Jesus being raised from the dead, which enabled all believers to be raised from the dead unto life. This made our salvation complete! We, being raised from spiritual death unto life, completed salvation. The Bible calls this change in us as being born again, a new creation. We received a new spirit that was created in righteousness and holiness and created by the Holy Word of God.

Being *born again* not of corruptible seed but of incorruptible [seed] by the word of God which liveth and abideth forever. (1 Peter 1:23, emphasis mine)

Our new birth (spirit) being created by the Holy Word of God in righteousness and holiness, there is no way that this new spirit has any sin in it. Besides, that is the reason God gave you a new spirit, because the spirit that you were born with by the seed of man had the sin of Adam in it.

Before you accepted Jesus for the forgiveness of your sin, you were spiritually dead. You were born of the seed of man with the sin of Adam. You were unrighteous, ruled by the lust of the flesh, and a sinner.

After you accepted Jesus Christ, you were forgiven of all sins and raised from being spiritually dead to spiritually alive.

For as in Adam all die so also in Christ all [those who believe in the cross of Christ] will be made alive. (1 Corinthians 15:22)

Therefore just as through one man [Adam] sin entered into the world [human race] and dead through sin and so death spread to *all* men because all have sinned. (Romans 5:12, emphasis mine)

Behold, I was brough forth [born] in iniquity [sin] and in my sin, my mother conceived me. (Psalm 51:5)

Remember where I told you that you received a new spirit? Here are the scriptures that support that:

A new heart will I give you and a *new spirit will I [God] put within you*; and I will take away the stony heart out of your flesh and give you a heart of flesh. (Ezekiel 36:26, emphasis mine)

And you put on the *new* man [your new spirit] which after God is created in righteousness and holiness. (Ephesians 4:24, emphasis mine)

The apostle Paul's revelation of the cross of Jesus talks about the "old man" and the "new man." The *old man* was the spirit that you were born with that had the sin of Adam. The *new man* was the new spirit that God put in you and was created by the Word of God.

The apostle Paul said that there are two persons in every believer. A person is a spirit, and a spirit is a person; they are the same. So you could say every believer has two persons in them or two spirits in them, and you would be saying the same thing.

What I just told you of the apostle Paul is the revelation of the cross of Jesus concerning the old man and the new man; the spirit of God simplified that revelation to me as two spirits. It is the same revelation because a person is a spirit and a spirit is a person. The spirit also gave me the scriptures that support the two spirits: the spirit that you were born with (Paul's old man) and the spirit that God put in us when we were born again (Paul's new man) (Ezekiel 36:26).

The spirit gave me this simplified revelation of the apostle Paul (it is the same but explained differently) and asked me, "What are you going to do with this simplicity of Paul's revelation that I gave you?"

I said to him, "What do you want me to do with it?"

The spirit of God said, "I want you to write it down and put it in a book."

I told the Lord, "I have never written a book in my life, and I wouldn't know how to get started."

He said, "I will help you from the beginning to the end."

So I got a pad, pen, and dictionary. And I said, "Where do we start?"

At the beginning. The garden of Eden. My first book was born. The title of my first book is *Every Christian Should Read This Book*. You can order it on Amazon. After reading this book, your knowledge is going to increase greatly, and you will know more about the Bible than you have in your lifetime.

Not too long ago (2019), I was diagnosed with multiple myeloma, which is a cancer of the blood. However, God knew that I knew what to do and how to do it. I knew what the Bible says of how to be healed of any disease by confessing God's healing promises in faith. I did that, and I was healed of this incurable disease. There is no sign of this disease in my blood.

I told the Lord, "Wouldn't it be great if my brothers and sisters in Christ knew how to be healed by your healing promises?"

He said, "Why don't you tell them?"

DISEASES

Diseases are killing God's people because they don't ask for help. The information that is in this book is going to heal thousands and thousands of people. This writing is dedicated to Christians, believers of the gospel of Jesus Christ. The reason it is not for nonbelievers is because they would not be able to believe in spiritual things anyway, and the words that I am going to share are very spiritual. A person who is not born again is carnal-minded, and spiritual revelations are foolishness to him.

But the natural man [nonbelievers] receives not the things of the Spirit of God, for they are foolishness to him. Neither can he know them because they are spiritually discerned [understood]. (1 Corinthians 2:14)

Statistics show that one out of four (4) people will have some type of cancer in their lifetime. Diseases are in the earth and are killing God's people when God has provided healing for them in his promises that are in the Bible. Christians have failed to connect to God's power.

With your help and a good attitude, we are going to change that, and you are going to be healed by the power of God's promise just as I was healed.

The healing process that I am going to show you is "not" complicated and is not something that you are not going to be able to understand.

Our medical science and institutions have gotten so good that they are able to deal with so many of the diseases that we have today. However, most of the time they need to catch the sickness in its early stages. Our great doctors are still limited. But Jesus, the source of all supernatural healing, is not limited. And his Word is not limited, and your faith is not limited.

Everyone's body is still under the curse of sin. If it wasn't under the curse, you would live forever. But it is, and your body is subject to sickness and diseases.

However, God knew we would need healing for our body, so he gave us healing promises to heal us. There is a time for all of us to leave this earth, but we are not going to let Satan take us before it's our time. The just shall live (not die) by faith (Hebrews 10:38).

Everything that I am going to tell you will be supported by Bible scriptures. Most churches do not teach the things that you are going to read in this book. I have studied the Bible for years and have listened to the New Testament seventy-plus times, and every teacher has a gift in some area of the Bible. My total interest was "faith." I read everything I could about faith. Faith is more than believing; it is how you believe— and that is Bible faith.

Sickness and disease came into the world when sin came into the world. You have been forgiven of all your sins and have been born again. You received a *new* spirit; you are a new creature. Your new spirit was created by the Word of God when you believed that Jesus paid the price for you on his cross and was raised from the dead (1 Peter 1:23).

You got saved; your body did not. It is subject to sickness and disease because of sin. Jesus paid the price for our healing with the stripes (beatings) he took from the Roman soldiers. We have a right to be healed. The Lord's Word will heal our body with our faith. Everything we receive from God is by faith!

They cried out to the Lord…and He [Lord] *sent his word* and healed them and delivered them from their destruction [grave]. (Psalm 107:19–20, emphasis mine)

For nonbelievers, if you are at a point in your life that you want to turn away from the way that you are living and be saved, I can help you. Say this scripture out loud:

If you shall confess with your mouth, the Lord Jesus and believe in your heart that God has raised Him from the dead, you shall be saved. (Romans 10:9)

What this means is that you believe that Jesus paid the price for your sins on the cross and was raised from the dead by God the Father, so you could be also raised from the dead unto life. By your faith in the crucifixion of Jesus, you are born again, a new creature, and received a new spirit with no sin that was created in righteousness and holiness. Too good to be true? God is that good, and he does not want anyone to go to hell. You will not feel any different at first, but give yourself a few weeks, and you will. You will have a new life. Also get my book *Every Christian Should Read This Book*. It tells you the whole story from beginning to the end, Adam and Eve and the cross of Jesus Christ.

If you want supernatural healing, you must go to the source—the source is the Word of God (Jesus Christ). Faith in the healing promises of God will not fail. Be patient, keep confessing the promise, and the manifestation of your healing will appear in your body.

Speak the promises daily, and your faith in the promises will get stronger and stronger, and the faith needed will be there. Then praise God for healing your body: not going to heal but has healed your disease. Remember the scripture says, "Believe you have received it and you shall have it" (Mark 11:24). This is God's method for not only healing believers but also answering your prayers. Bible faith is believing you receive it, and then you shall have it.

Bible faith is not speaking the problem or confessing the problem—it is speaking or confessing the answer to the problem. When you do this, your faith gives substance to God's promise by planting the promise in your newborn spirit, which is capable to bring the promise into manifestation in your physical body.

GOD THE FATHER AND THE LORD JESUS CHRIST

God resides in the spiritual world. There are two worlds: the physical and the spiritual. The spiritual is so much greater because the spiritual made or created everything you see in the physical.

God is *not* ordinary, and his Word is not ordinary. God is capable of doing supernatural things for us who believe, and healing your diseases is just one of many. The Bible says that the Word of God is above everything, even above the name of Jesus. So, if you (Christians) need a miracle or supernatural healing, I am going to tell you how to get it in this book. God asked me to write this book to help Christians.

God is going to bring a healing to his people in this country and throughout the whole world that we have never seen before. The healing ministry of Jesus got people's attention, and they believed in Christ. There is going to be another wave of the healing ministry of Jesus.

The healer is Jesus Christ, and he is the One who is going to heal you by his Word (promises of God) mixed with *your* faith.

The more we know about someone, particularly if the information we receive is all good, the more confidence we will have in that person. The Bible gives us a lot of information about God, so let's look at some of the things that the Bible says.

1. *God is the Creator* of all things. Everything that is made was made by him: the earth, the sea with all that is in it, the animals, the birds, all the planets that exist, the angels, and the human race (John 1:3).

2. The full greatness of God is beyond our understanding, but we still can know a great deal about our Creator.

3. *The love of God*—He created us for himself, and his love for us is forever.

4. *God is forgiving*, and his mercy for us is great.

5. *God has always existed*; he has no beginning and no end.

6. *God is holy* and hates sin. All sin must be paid for, and Jesus did that for us on the cross.

7. *God is all-powerful*, just, slow to anger, and a jealous God, jealous for us.

8. *God is a faith God* and a spirit. We are a spirit—he made us after his kind. We are a spirit with a soul and live in a body of flesh. To please God one must have faith in him and believe his Word.

9. *God cannot lie.* That is why God's promises are true and yes and Amen. Christians, remember this one, because it is the key to your healing. God's promises have already been provided, and all you have to do is accept them.

Here are some more Bible scriptures about the Lord and who he is:

I am the Lord and there is no other; apart from me, there is no God. (Isaiah 45:5)

Awesome! Wow! Does that scripture tell you who God is? He made us, he loves us, and he has the power to help and heal us from any—yes, I said any—disease that comes upon us. But we have a part to play. That part is to believe and have faith in God's promises.

How to have Bible faith may not be exactly what you might think. Bible faith is what I am going to explain to you in this book. I will go over this with you so there will not be any mistake on how to believe God's way and what the Bible says.

The Lord Almighty, blessed is the one who trusts in you. (Psalm 84:12)

The Lord is gracious and righteous, full of compassion. (Psalm 116:5)

The Lord is not slow in keeping His promises as some understand slowness. (2 Peter 3:9)

God is not human that he should lie, not a human that He should change His mind. Does He promise and not fulfill? (*No!*) (Numbers 23:19)

What is impossible with men is possible with God. (Luke 18:27)

For you Lord is good and ready to forgive and merciful unto all them that call on Him. (Psalm 86:5)

The Lord, your redeemer, who formed you from the womb: I am the Lord who made all things. (Isaiah 44:24)

Remember the former things of old; for I am God and there is no other. I am God and there is none like me. (Isaiah 46:9)

This is powerful! I hope you are getting a good understanding of who our Heavenly Father is.

Lord my God, I called to you for help and you healed me.

And when you call on him for help, he will heal you! (Believeth?) (Psalm 30:2)

Worship the Lord your God. I will take away sickness from among you. (Exodus 23:25)

Bless the Lord O my soul and forget not all his *benefits* who forgives all our iniquities [sins] and *heals all* our diseases. (Psalm 103:2–3, emphasis mine)

It is very important that you have a good understanding of who God is. I have given you a lot of information about your Heavenly Father. You can trust him. You should tell him you love him. He is not some spiritual being who is in heaven and does not have any idea of what is going on in your life. The Lord knows everything that is going on with you and cares! You have a "free will," so he is waiting for you to call on him for help and anything else that you need. If you have neglected him in the past, reconnect with him. It is not how we start the race in life; it is how we finish the race.

Having a connection with God is the best security one could have. You are important to him. Make him important to you!

FAITH

What is faith?

Now faith is the substance of things hoped for, the evidence of things not seen. (Hebrews 11:1)

There is a lot to say about faith. First of all, faith is the "only" avenue to God and the spiritual world where he is. Without faith, you could not be saved! So pay attention to everything I write down concerning faith, for it is through faith that you were saved. Faith came after Jesus paid the price for sin on the cross. Faith replaced the law (Ten Commandments), because Jesus fulfilled the law on the cross.

Faith gives substance to all the blessings of God. Faith brings into manifestation what you are requesting or praying for. So the promises of God are yes, and not maybe, with faith.

Christians sometimes get hoping and believing mixed up. They think that they are the same thing. They are not. Hoping for something is in the future. Faith is believing you have it *now*. Hoping does not give substance; faith does. People who do not know God's will, will say

1. If it is God's will, it will come. If it is not his will, I will not receive.

2. Sometimes God answers prayer with yes, no, or not at this time.

Sorry. I know this sounds religious, but it is not true. The Word, the promise, is God's will. God has a lot of confidence in the born-again Christian. Would a Christian ask for a lot of money so he could indulge in his own selfish desires? He better go back to the cross of Jesus and start over.

Don't think God would handle things as we would. He is more generous, loving, forgiving, and everything else that's good than we are! However, God must be first in our lives, and prayer must be based on the Word.

What things you desire when you pray *believe that you have received them and you shall have them.* (Mark 11:24, emphasis mine) And forgive others.

God's Word offers you more than your needs met. It offers your desires, healing for your body, and whatever else the Word says. But the key is faith—believing that you have what you are asking for *now*. Do you have it now? No. But *Bible faith is believing that you have it now*—and then with patience you will receive it.

There is another word that is important in faith. That word is *expecting*.

Here is King David who knew about faith:

In the morning, Lord you hear my voice; in the morning I lay my request before you and wait *expectantly*. (Psalm 5:3, emphasis mine)

He was waiting expectantly because he believed his request would be answered—not yes, no, or not at this time. The promises of God are yes. Your requests must be based on the Word of God.

King David knew the key of faith. Make your request in faith and wait, "expecting" your request to be answered. Once a Christian gets the understanding of faith and uses the understanding, he glorifies God. Our Father is a faith God. He knows you have been saved and changed to the likeness of Jesus Christ and are a giver and not a taker, kind, and compassionate and have a spirit of power, love, and a sound mind. And he wants to give you what you need and desire. When Jesus went to the cross and rose from the dead, you were forgiven and became a new person, born again. The kingdom of heaven is now on the earth *in* every believer of Jesus Christ.

And God blessed the seventh day and sanctified it because that in it he had rested from all his work which God *created* and *made*. (Genesis 2:3, emphasis mine)

Everything that is made was made out of what was already created.

Everything that was created was created by a seed.

In the physical world, we create things from a seed. If you want corn, you plant a corn seed in the ground. If you want oranges, you plant orange seeds in the ground, and you get orange trees that grow oranges. Everything that does not exist is created by a seed. If you want oranges, you don't plant pear seeds and hope to get oranges.

Everything produces *after its kind*. Think about that. Lions produce lions, and tigers produce tigers, after their kind. But everything that is created is created from a seed.

Another person might say, "I got two areas of good land. I am going to plant orange seeds and get some orange trees." He plants without getting any instruction on *how* to plant, how deep to plant, when to water, etc. So nothing happens, and he wonders why.

He did not take the time to get instructions on *how to do this*. He knew *what* to do but did not know *how*. This book is going to teach you "what" to plant and "how" to plant to receive the healing for your body.

Now, let's discuss the spiritual world and how it works. There are a lot of similarities with the physical world, but they are different. In the spiritual realm, everything that is created is created by a seed and faith. Guess what the seeds are? Are you ready for this? Words. Words are the seeds that are used to create. God created everything that you see in the physical world with his Word. His Word was the seed. Since he made us in his image and likeness and everything produces after its kind, our words are seeds and if spoken in faith will create what was spoken. The difference is that God never ever speaks foolishness or negative words like we do, so he has written in his Word to educate us. We have been bringing bad things in our life by what we have been saying and believing. We were ignorant of this spiritual law. Here are some Bible scriptures that support what I just told you. Remember what is in your spirit (heart) in abundance will come out of your mouth.

A good man [believers] out of the good treasure of his heart brings forth that which is good; and an evil man out of the evil treasure of his heart brings forth that which is evil; for the abundance of the heart his mouth speaks. (Luke 6:45)

This is pretty easy to understand. How are the above persons bringing things forth? By speaking them! They both brought forth good or bad things into their lives by speaking them and believing what they spoke.

If any man among you seems to be religious and bridle not his tongue, but deceives his own heart [spirit], this man's religion is vain. (James 1:26)

A nonbeliever is not going to believe that scripture, but you better believe it, or your life on earth is going to be filled with problems. Christians have enough problems from the devil without adding to them. However, he is the one who's getting you to say these negative sayings to bring on these problems. Well, I'm just saying it like it is. Start saying it like you want it and change the problem that exists. This is more important than you might think:

I [God] create the fruit [what you say] of the lips; Peace, peace to him that is far off and to him that is near, saith the Lord, and I will heal him. (Isaiah 57:19)

God creates the fruit of your lips. What are you going to say? How sick you are and it is getting worse? Or are you going to say, "Your word in Psalm 103, Lord, says you have forgiven me of all my sins and healed *all* my diseases! I accept your word and thank you for healing all my diseases! Thank you, Lord. I believe and say with my mouth I am now healed"?

Pay attention to what I am going to say here. When you have a disease, you do not say, "I don't have this disease. I don't have this disease." That is not what you confess! You don't deny that you have the disease, because you do. What you are doing by speaking the promise is confessing healing to *replace* the disease and to make you well. This is supernatural but *true*.

One more thing while I'm talking about believing. Because you see the healing scripture in the Bible and you believe it is true, you must get that healing scripture *inside you; and you do that by speaking the scripture out loud and believing it*. When you speak the healing promise in faith, *you plant* the promise in your new spirit. Then you keep confessing God's promise and wait, *expecting* your healing to come. This is God's method and God's way of healing you. Have confidence in God's love for you and the power of his Word.

Very, very important: Believing or not believing is simply a choice that you make. It is not a matter of having great faith or little faith. It is a matter of choice. I choose to believe. Do you?

Thou shall also decree a thing and it shall be established unto you.

What you decree, whatever you keep saying in faith, will come to you, good or bad. (Job 22:28)

A fool's mouth is his destruction and his lips [speaking] are the snare of his soul. (Proverbs 18:7)

There are many more, but I'm sure you get the point. Don't disregard these words of wisdom, but give thought to them. Be the most positive- minded person you have ever been. Speaking words in faith and receiving is a spiritual law.

(God speaking) My people are destroyed for a lack of knowledge. (You are not one of them now!) (Hosea 4:6)

Now I have given you the knowledge of what not to do. Do you have ears to hear?

Very important: Faith is believing you will receive your request now.

Then wait, expecting.

God never created anything without saying it first. His words were the seed, and God is full of faith.

Our born-again spirit was created by our faith in believing the Word of God that Jesus Christ died for us and rose from the dead. In brief, the Bible says that we were born again of the incorruptible seed, the Word of God. The Bible calls Jesus the Word of God. So, with our faith in the Word of God, we are a new creation, a new creature, and have all the attributes of Jesus Christ. And as we mature and grow, we will get closer to the likeness of Jesus. How do we grow? By increasing in the knowledge of the Word, which is also causing our faith to get stronger and grow.

Now let's discuss how faith comes or increases.

So then faith comes from hearing and hearing by the Word of God. (Romans 10:17)

Some Christians might question if they have the faith to believe God's promises for their healing. Regardless of the level of your faith, it can be increased. Romans 10:17 says that faith comes (increases) from hearing and hearing God's Word. To hear God's Word, it must be spoken. You must speak God's promise of healing out loud so you can hear it. Read it slowly and think about every word. God is the One who is saying it. God cannot lie, and all the promises are *yes—not maybe.*

Nobody knows your body better than God. He made our body out of the dust of the ground. You trusted the Lord for your salvation. Now trust him for your healing! Trusting and believing are simply making a decision to believe. It is up to you. God's Word has the power to make heaven and earth; it's certainly got the power to heal your body.

When you confess the healing promise out loud, you *plant* the seed (promise) in your spirit. When the seed gets in your spirit, in time it will manifest itself in your physical body, and healing is the result.

Believe you have received it, and you shall have it. God's method is to *believe first.* Then you will receive.

Stand firm in your faith, because the devil is coming. We cannot keep the devil from bringing doubt in our mind. When these doubts come, start praising God for your healing, and he will leave. Be prepared and fight him, by "praising God." God is glorified when you are believing his Word. Be strong, have courage by believing God's Word, and glorify your Lord, Jesus Christ.

How to Activate the Promises of God to Heal Your Body

There is an abundance of diseases in this world: different types of cancer, Parkinson's, and so many more. But it doesn't make any difference. God's promise of healing has the power to heal you from any one of them. Also, use the name of Jesus against your disease: "In the name of Jesus Christ, I am healed of _____, and my body has been made whole. Thank you, Lord!" The name of Jesus is above every name.

If anyone has been diagnosed with any disease, fatal or not, you need this knowledge on how and what to do. It does not matter what disease it is. The healing process is the same. Again, I am telling you to go to your doctor and go through any treatments that they recommend but also do the teaching of this book. It is easy, it is in the Bible, and it will heal your body.

If you were diagnosed with a fatal disease, here are your options:

1. Take only the treatment from your doctor and die slowly.

2. Follow the teaching of the Bible in this book and live by doing both.

Let me ask you some questions:

1. Do you believe God's Word has power?

2. Do you believe God's Word has the creative power to change things?

If God is giving you his Word, then he is giving you his power that will change anything that you point it at—in this case, healing for your body. There should be no doubt on your part of what God's Word can do, but you have a part in your healing. Your part is making a choice to believe God's promise. Spiritual believing works this way: believing God's promise that says you are healed, *accepting* God's promise, and confessing it out loud, "Thank you, Lord Jesus, for healing me of this disease. I accept your Word and the healing power that is in your Word." Say it slowly, out loud five- plus times in the morning and at night. Again, you are not confessing that you do not have this disease!

Bless the Lord O my soul and forget not all his *benefits* who forgives all our iniquities [sins]; who heals *all* our diseases. (Psalm 103:2–3, emphasis mine)

This is God's Word coming out of the mouth of King David. King David spoke with God continually, and God shared with him about faith.

God's promise has the creative power to change what exists. Do you believe that? The only other thing that is needed is your faith, believing the promise. If you have a fatal or nonfatal disease, God's Word with your faith can replace your disease with health, by speaking

God's promise out loud and—this is important—*accepting* God's Word that you are *now* healed. From that moment on your saying is this: "I am healed by the power of God's Word. Thank you, Lord, for healing me of all my diseases and forgiving me of all my sins." Speak this every day and at night. I am going to tell you this so you will not be caught off guard.

Beware that the devil is going to pay you a visit in your mind. He (devil) might send your sweet neighbor to see how you are doing to get you to say that you still have the disease through a conversation. Your sweet neighbor will have no idea that he or she is being used by the devil. If that happens when you are by yourself, repeat this to the Lord and then watch over your mouth in the future. You must stand firm in what you are believing and confessing. Also, how you *feel* has nothing to do with what you are believing. The devil could give you a pain, and you might say, "I thought I was healed?" You are basing how you feel on what you believe. You will feel better later but not at the beginning. However, keep believing, keep confessing that you are healed in the name of Jesus, and you will receive.

The big question is, "How long do I have to wait before I hear the doctor's good news?" The Bible does not give us any time. That will depend on each individual. Be patient and stand firm in what you are saying and believing. Relax and have confidence in your merciful, forgiving Lord.

If you are filled with anxiety and full of worry, that is a "red flag," and you are not there (faith). If you are believing God's promise, then a *peace* will come over you. You will not be afraid. You must do your part, and don't try to figure out how the Lord is going to do his. Your objective is to be healed, and you don't care how the Lord is going to bring it to pass. The Lord has many options. When you get your good news, make sure you thank him and praise him for giving back your well-being! What I just told you might sound supernatural, but that is exactly what it is. It is supernatural because God is supernatural. But it is yours if you want it. It was easy for me because my faith was highly developed. But a person does not need real strong faith to get their healing. Just believe in God and his Word, and you are there. If a person needed real strong faith, then I would *not* be writing this book. Again, just make the choice to believe.

Now, I am going to take you to a new subject that happened to us when Jesus went to the cross, was crucified, and was raised from the dead. We all know that was for forgiveness of our sins and us being changed into a new creature—born again. Jesus also destroyed the work of the devil, which was *sin in us*. Jesus paid the price or wages of our sin, which enabled God to forgive all who believed him. The believers being forgiven of all sins, it broke the power of sin over us and set us free from the power of sin.

The "cross of Jesus" also brought judgment on the devil and the angels that followed him, and they were kicked out of heaven.

> And there was war in Heaven. Michael and his angels fought against the dragon [devil] and the dragon fought and his angels prevailed not; neither was their place found anymore in Heaven. And the great dragon was cast out; that old serpent called the Devil and Satan which deceiveth the whole world. He was cast out into the earth and his angels were cast out with him. And I heard a loud voice saying in Heaven: Now has come salvation and strength and the kingdom of our God and the power of His Christ; for the accuser of our brethren is cast down which accused them before our God day and night. (Revelation 12:7–10)

The cross of Jesus also brought the kingdom of God in heaven to the earth only for the believers of Jesus Christ.

And when he was demanded of the Pharisees when the kingdom of God should come, he answered them and said: the kingdom of God cometh not with observation. Neither shall they say lo here or lo there; for behold the kingdom of God is *within you*. (Luke 17:20– 21, emphasis mine)

The kingdom of God that is in heaven is now on the earth after Jesus went to the cross. It is in every believer of the cross of Jesus Christ. The new born-again spirit that God put in every believer is in the kingdom of God on earth (Luke 17:20–21).

Now, let me take you to a very important Bible scripture about "how the kingdom of God on earth works."

So is the kingdom of God, as if a man should cast seed in the ground. And he should sleep and rise night and day and the seed should spring and grow up, he knows not how. (Mark 4:26–27)

In this scripture, the Bible is telling us how the Word (promise) of God works here on earth.

Here is the spiritual revelation of this scripture:

1. The man cast seed—The man is speaking or confessing God's Word.

2. The seed—That is, God's Word.

3. The ground—That is, man's spirit.

4. Man slept night and day—The man is waiting patiently.

5. Seed should spring and grow up—That is the manifestation of the Word (promise) of God to the believer.

When the seed gets in the ground or when the Word of God gets in your spirit, it is a done deal. If you wait and don't give up, you will receive: one more thing, when you are confessing God's Word, it *plants* the Word of God in your spirit. Faith carries the word of promise to your born-again spirit, which is capable of producing what comes in—good or bad. So confess God's Word, and good things will happen. And you will say, "Why didn't I know this years ago?" You may have but never did it. Nothing happens until the Word is planted!

Let me make this perfectly clear. This method of God will not happen just because you are confessing his promise. You must speak his Word in faith (believing). If you confess God's Word over and over, faith will come if you are willing. Just say, "I am going to believe God's promise!" You got to want to believe it!

I am now going to give you many healing scriptures for you to use. Before you get started, I strongly suggest that you reread this faith chapter of the book two or three times and make notes of what you need to do. This method is supernatural, but there is nothing normal with God the Father and our Lord Jesus Christ. He made "everything" that is made including us, the human race. Don't downplay the power of God. He loves you and wants to help you in whatever you need and has the power to do it. Do you believe that?

God loved us first. Let us return our love back to him by telling him how much we love him and appreciate him. Don't be afraid of anything, not even death. Let your love for God cast out all fear. Trust him with your life. I did. These healing scriptures that I am giving you are many. All you need is two. I will show you "how" to use them for your healing. Read these scriptures out loud as many times as it takes to get faith to believe.

Remember God has already said "yes" to them.

I [God] created the fruit of the lips; peace, peace to him that is far off and to him that is near says the Lord; and I will heal him. (Isaiah 57:19)

What the Lord is saying here is "What you are saying [confessing] in faith with your mouth, I will create it, and you will be healed." So ask, accept, and then praise him for your healing. Clean your conscience by repenting!

Bless the Lord O my soul and forget not all his *benefits* who forgives all our iniquities [sins]; who heals *all* our diseases. (Psalm 103:2–3 [I used this one], emphasis mine)

When you pray, read this scripture out loud to the Lord. "Your Word is true, and I *accept* and believe that you have forgiven me of all my sins and healed all my diseases, including _____, and I say that I am healed by the power of your Word. Thank you, Lord, for healing me." (Believe you have received your healing *now*, not going to sometime in the future.)

And whatsoever you shall ask [the Father] in my name that will I do that the Father may be glorified in the Son. (John 14:13)

"Father God, in the name of Jesus, I ask to be healed of all my diseases, including the disease I was diagnosed with, _____. Jesus said he would do the healing to glorify you. Thank you, Lord, for healing me and making my body whole." Speak this out loud daily.

And all things you ask in prayer, believing, you will receive. (Matthew 21:22)

Always read the Bible verse back to the Lord out loud and then say, "I ask you, Lord, to be healed. And I believe that all promises are yes and Amen. Than you, Lord, for healing me. And therefore I say I am healed *now* according to your word in Matthew 21:22." Speak this every day.

Who His [Jesus] own self bare our sins in His own body on the tree, that we being dead to sins, should live unto righteousness by whose stripes you were healed. (By the stripes of Jesus, I believe I am healed.) (1 Peter 2:24)

These things I have spoken unto you, that in me you might have peace. In the world you shall have tribulation; but, be of good cheer, for I have overcome the world. (John 16:33)

For whosoever is born of God [saved] overcomes the world; and this is the victory that overcomes the world—our faith. (1 John 5:4)

John 16:33 and 1 John 5:4 Bible scriptures go together. What is the Lord saying in these two Bible verses?

The Lord is saying this: no matter what suffering or distress the world brings, be of good cheer, because you can overcome it. How? By your *faith* in the Word of God. This includes sickness and diseases.

When you study the New Testament, you are going to find out that with (1) your faith and (2) God's Word you are able to overcome anything that is undesirable in this world.

Because of our sins being removed by faith in Christ and us being born again, our Father God sees us blameless in his sight and is willing to use his power on our behalf.

The righteous cry out and the Lord hears them; He delivers them from all their troubles. (Psalm 34:17)

Never claim ownership to any sickness or disease that you were diagnosed with—"my disease" or "my sickness." When you pray to the Lord, speak of the healing that you are requesting: "by his stripes you are healed." Healing is God's will for you—believing is a decision that you make to be healed, and only you can make it. Nobody can make it for you. I was healed of cancer of the blood by doing these things that I am sharing with you.

You [Jesus] restored me to health and let me live. Surely, it was for my benefit that I suffered such anguish. In your love you kept me from the pit of destruction; you have put all my sins behind your back. (Isaiah 38:16–17)

This is really an eye-opener. The great prophet Isaiah was sick and at the point of death, and Jesus healed him. It goes to show us that we all are subject to sickness and disease. However, we can overcome it. How? With our faith in the promises of God.

I say to you and with your faith in God's word you will be healed just as I was healed, no might be but will be. All you need to do is make a decision to believe God's promise. You do not need strong faith to make a decision. It is a choice you make, and then wait, "expecting" for good news from your doctor. Remember Bible faith is believing you are healed *now*, and then you will receive the promise, healing. If you have any unforgiveness with anyone or anything else, repent and accept God's forgiveness and move on in faith. God loves you and wants to heal you. You are his!

Let me give you an example of how you should think about your newly diagnosed disease.

Let's say that you suddenly get a "cold." You know from the start that this cold will go away in time, so you believe that this cold will be gone in a few weeks right from the start.

This is the same mindset you should have about the disease that came on your body. Right from the start you know that God's promise is more powerful than this disease and will make it disappear with your faith. There is no disease that God's Word cannot remove with your faith. This is spiritual and available to "all" Christians.

I guess I had to go through this terrible experience of being diagnosed with multiple myeloma, an incurable disease. The doctors call it an incurable disease because they have never found a cure for it. But the Lord has a cure for it or any other disease: it is his healing promises (his Word) that are in the Bible, accepted by believers in faith, spoken out loud. Once his Word goes into your spirit, it is planted. You water the seed by praising God for your healing before there is any evidence that has taken place.

But the manifestation is evident and will appear in your physical body. Praise and give thanks to the Lord for he is "good," forgiving and merciful.

Believers, don't pass on this healing process that God has provided for us. Why would you? It is ours, a gift from God. By the way, when you are healed, tell as many Christians as you can every day of your remaining years.

God's Word spoken out of your mouth in faith is the answer to your health.

Again, believe God's healing promises, speak his promises out loud every day, and thank him for healing you and expect your healing to be manifested in your body. It took me two months and two weeks before the doctors saw a big improvement with my blood test. So be patient and be confident. *Do not fear!* Believe you are healed *now*, when you accepted God's healing promises. In the physical world, when you plant a "good seed" in good ground, you cannot see anything that is happening below the ground. Does that mean that nothing is happening?

It is God's will to heal, but only the ones who decide to believe will be healed. What is your decision?

RENEWING YOUR MIND WITH THE WORD

The Bible tells us that we need to renew our minds with the Word of God. We live in the physical world, and our mind is physically minded. The mind knows very little about spiritual things. When we make known the spiritual things to the mind, then the mind will accept them. Otherwise, the mind will fight to resist. Your spirit controls the mind, and the mind controls the body. The born-again spirit I am talking about. Your new spirit now controls the tongue, whereas before you accepted Christ, the devil controlled you and your tongue. I know the Bible says that no man can control his tongue, but that was before you got saved. Romans 7:19–25 talks about that, and at the end it says, "Oh what a wretched man I am; who shall deliver me from this body of death? I thank God through Jesus Christ our Lord."

When you got saved, you were forgiven of all sins, and sin lost all power over you, including the devil. You have been set free by faith in the power of Jesus's cross and his resurrection.

It is very important to get your mind renewed to spiritual things, so I am going to cherry-pick some Bible scriptures that will accomplish that very thing.

You will get your mind renewed and gain much-needed knowledge at the same time. I strongly suggest that *you meditate on each scripture* and learn what each scripture is saying. Have faith and believe these scriptures, but most of all, use them in your everyday life. Everything that you need in this life is provided in the Bible. But you must plant these verses in your spirit by faith, by confessing/speaking these Bible verses out loud so the seed (promise) will get in your spirit.

Nothing happens until the seed is planted! Believe. Plant the promise by speaking it out loud, and with patience, then you will receive the manifestation of the promise. This is God's method.

When Jesus Christ came into the world, he went to the cross, was crucified, and was raised from the dead. He paid the price that God demanded for our sins. We received the forgiveness of our sin by faith in the works of the cross and were born again and received a new spirit, with no sin in it. We are a new creature, created by the Word of God of what Jesus did for us! It was by faith in Christ that we received this grace from God the Father. It was God's love for us that he sent Jesus Christ to the cross (Ezekiel 36:26).

God gave us a *new spirit*, soul, and conscience—a completely new person. God did not give us a new spirit of fear but of power, love, and a sound mind.

If we confess our sin, He is faithful and just to forgive us our sin and cleanse us from all unrighteousness. (1 John 1:9)

All Christians do some wrong things in life. When you do acknowledge these wrongs, repent right away and don't wait. Keep your conscience clean, and your faith will remain strong.

Now, faith is the substance of things hoped [requested] for, the evidence of things not seen. (Hebrews 11:1)

Faith brings the thing that you are hoping for to you. Believe you have received it *now*.

All Christians *must* be forgivers of others. This is not a suggestion; if you do not forgive, your faith will fail. Let bad people's words slide off your back like water does off a duck. Do not let anything control you, except the Holy Spirit. You want to please God and not "busybodies." Have that mindset.

If any of you lack wisdom, let him ask God that give to all men [Christians] liberally and it shall be given to him. But let him ask in faith, not wavering [doubting]. For that man shall not receive anything from the Lord. (James 1:5–8)

Knowing about faith is the only way to receive from God. When you ask, then you believe you received—and hold on and don't let go of that promise. The promises have been provided for you. All you do is accept them.

But without faith, it is *impossible* to please God. (Hebrews 11:6, emphasis mine)

Without faith, God cannot help you. Why do you think the devil is always trying to get you to doubt? Be a believer!

So then Faith comes [increases] by hearing and hearing by the word of God. (Romans 10:17)

The scripture below does not say yes, no, or not at this time. People are trying to put themselves in God's place. Pray, ask, believe, and receive.

God wants you to pray, ask, and receive. He wants you to develop your faith in him, to get stronger and stronger in life. Have a believing mindset!

And *all* things whatsoever you shall ask in prayer, believing, you shall receive. (If you hold on and don't give up.) (Matthew 21:22, emphasis mine)

Unto you, it is given to know the mystery of the Kingdom of God, but unto those [unbelievers] that are without nothing is given. (Mark 4:11)

To know the mystery is to know the unknown. And it has been given to us. What is it? Coming up in this next scripture is telling us the unknown.

(Jesus talking) So is the Kingdom of God as if a man should cast seed in the ground. And he should sleep and rise night and day and the *seed* should spring and grow up, he knows not how. (Mark 4:26–27)

This scripture tells us how the kingdom of God works and also how faith works. And the two, faith and the kingdom of God, go together.

The scripture says, "And man should cast seed in the ground." The revelation is that man speaks out loud the Word of God, which is the seed. Man plants the Word of God into man's spirit, which is the ground, and sleeps night and day—man waits for the Word to grow and manifest itself to the believer.

That is how faith works and how the kingdom of God works. The Word of God spoken in faith goes into your spirit and in time produces back to the believer. This is God's method in the spiritual. Similarly, as a man plants a seed in the ground, in time, it grows up and produces whatever the seed is in the physical world.

This is how we can overcome sickness and disease in our body by confessing out loud the healing promise of God with faith, and the healing promise goes in our spirit and produces healing in our body. That's what I did, and healing came, and the disease that was incurable became curable and disappeared. This is why I am writing this book, to get you to reconnect with the healing power in God's promises. Remember that believing is receiving the Lord's healing promise now and not going to later. Believe you have received it, and you shall have it.

I [God] create the fruit of the lips. (Isaiah 57:19)

God creates what you say in faith, good or bad! God says that his Word will not return to him void. Before I get finished with this book, you are going to realize that you better be more focused on the words you speak. This is the mystery of the kingdom of God, and that is why this is revealed to us and not to the world. The Lord wanted this to work for you and not against you.

Here are some Bible scriptures that support what I just told you, coming from King Solomon in Proverbs:

The mouth of the upright shall deliver them. (Proverbs 12:6) The lips of the wise shall preserve them. (Proverbs 14:3)

He that keepeth his mouth keepeth his life. (Proverbs 13:3) The tongue of the wise is health. (Proverbs 12:18)

A man shall be satisfied with good by the fruit of his mouth. (Proverbs 12:14)

I sure hope you are starting to understand what the Lord wanted me to teach you in this book. Getting control over your mouth is imperative for your well-being.

He [Father God] that spared not His own son, but delivered Him [Jesus] up for us all, how shall He not with Him also freely give us [believers] all things? (Romans 8:32)

The love of God and the generosity of God is all over the Bible.

The thief [devil] comes to steal, kill and destroy; I [Jesus], have come that you might have life and have it more abundantly. (John 10:10)

Important to know: Anything that falls under steal, kill, and destroy belongs to the devil. Jesus wants to enhance your life with more than enough—abundance.

Whatsoever things you desire when you pray, believe that you [have] received them and you shall have them and when you stand praying, forgive if you have ought against any. (Mark 11:24–25)

We all have had someone do us wrong in some way. However, God is a forgiving spirit, and he *demands* us to be the same. Not forgiving hinders our faith in receiving the blessings of God and also robs us of our peace and joy in life. So forgive by faith, and don't believe the famous lie of the devil that one must forgive and forget. You can't forget, because you have a memory—you might not think about it, but it is still there.

The prayer of a righteous person is *powerful* and *effective*. (James 5:16, emphasis mine)

A righteous person? You are righteous by faith in Jesus Christ, so your prayers are powerful and effective. Let that sink in! Believe that because the Bible says so! All people who believe in the cross of Jesus Christ for the forgiveness of their sins and believe that he was raised from the dead are righteous.

Praise the Lord O my soul and forget not all His benefits; who forgives *all* your sins and heals *all* your diseases. (Psalm 103:2–3, emphasis mine)

The emphasis of this book is on healing, and the above scripture is one of the better ones to use for your confession.

Suggestion: Lord, you said out of the mouth of King David that you have forgiven us of all our sins and healed all our diseases. I accept your healing of the disease I was diagnosed with, and I have faith in your word, faith in Psalm 103. I confess that I am healed by the word of the Lord. Thank you, Lord Jesus." That is your confession daily. Bible faith is believing you have it *now*—not going to.

For whoever would love life and see good days, must keep their tongue from evil and their lips from deceitful speech. (1 Peter 3:10)

Your peace, joy, blessing from God, etc. all depend on your faith and your mouth (the words you speak).

Casting all your cares on Him [Jesus] because He cares for you. (1 Peter 5:7)

I cannot tell you how many times I have used this scripture when I became overwhelmed with problems. I would say: "Lord, this problem is too much for me to handle, so I am casting this problem over to you, for your word says that you care for me." When you do that, let the problem go—you gave it to Jesus to work it out, so let it go and wait. I have "never" been disappointed.

For God gave us a spirit not of fear, but of *power* and *love* and a *sound mind.* (2 Timothy 1:7, emphasis mine)

This spirit in the above scripture is the new spirit that you received from God when you were born again because of your faith in the cross of Jesus, when he was raised from the dead. When you accepted Christ and his resurrection, you received a new spirit (born again) with no sin in it.

A new heart also will I give you and a *new* spirit will I [God] put within you. (Ezekiel 36:26, emphasis mine)

Therefore, since we have been justified through *faith*, we have peace with God through our Lord Jesus Christ. (Romans 5:1)

In every scripture that you are going to read, faith is involved somehow.

In the morning, Lord, you hear my voice; in the morning I lay my requests before you and wait expectantly. (Psalm 5:3)

The key word here is *expectantly*. If King David was expectantly waiting, he was believing that God would answer his request. God wants his children to lean on him in faith. He is there for us because of our faith in Jesus Christ.

I am the way, the truth and the life; no man cometh to the Father, but by me [Jesus]. (John 14:6)

To go to heaven, one must be forgiven—and Jesus is the only forgiveness of sins.

The just shall live by faith. (Faith in what? The Word of God.) (Romans 1:17)

Holding the mystery [the unknown] of the faith in a pure conscience. (1 Timothy 3:9)

For a person who is in unforgiveness or doing things that are wrong, his conscience will condemn him and hinder his faith. To clean your conscience, you must repent and turn away from wrongdoings and be a forgiver. Know whom you became—a new person.

Delight yourself in the Lord and He shall give you the desires of your heart. *Commit* your way unto the Lord and trust in Him and He will bring it to pass. (Psalm 37:4–5, emphasis mine)

For the eyes of the Lord are over the righteous and His ears are open to their prayers. (1 Peter 3:12)

Some Christians think, *If I don't need something, I don't need to pray.* God's spirit is inside you. He wants to be a big part of your life. We are all faced with decisions in life—ask him and wait for the answer. Somehow, you'll know that is the thing to do when the answer comes. Increase your prayer life.

And by Him [Jesus], all that believe are justified from *all* things [sin] from which you could not be justified by the law of Moses. (The Ten Commandments) (Acts 13:39, emphasis mine)

For unto us was the gospel preached, as well as unto them. But, the word preached did not profit them not being mixed with faith to them that heard it. (Hebrews 4:2)

God's Word only profits those who believe it.

For the things which I greatly feared has come to me and that which I was afraid of has come unto me. (Job 3:25)

One better pay attention to this scripture. Fear will bring bad things to you, like faith will bring good things to you. Worry, stress, and fear are not out of our control. We have power over these emotions. It's just a matter of making a decision to resist these emotions, knowing that they are from the evil one. Do not fear when something bad happens. It will hinder your thinking and judgment. Keep calm and do what needs to be done and ask the Holy Spirit to help you. He is right there beside you. Where faith is, there is no fear.

A good man [a believer] out of the good treasure of his heart [spirit] brings forth that which is good; and an evil man [nonbeliever] out of the evil treasure of his heart lunges forth that which is evil. For of the abundance of the heart [spirit] his mouth speaks. (Luke 6:45)

Any believer not having this knowledge will speak evil on himself and have no idea of why bad things are happening. The above Bible verse reveals this knowledge to Christians. There are many scriptures in the Bible that say the same thing. The words that come out of your mouth *in faith* are powerful. This is how Satan controls nonbelievers—by getting them to speak negative things about themselves and enticing one to do evil.

The Lord is far from the wicked, but He hears the prayer of the righteous. (Proverbs 15:29)

This is your confidence that the Lord hears your prayers. Another Bible verse says: if the Lord hears us, then we have what we asked for. When one prays, you acknowledge God and show faith in him. He'll prove that your faith is not in vain.

Submit yourself to God. Resist the Devil and he will flee from you. (James 4:7)

The Bible says to resist the devil and he will flee from you. Do not get in a conversation with him. He is smarter than you, not greater. When you reveal to him that you know he's there, he will leave because he lost his cover. He wants you to think that the "thoughts" he puts in your head are "yours." So when you resist him, the devil knows that you know that it is him. The apostle Paul said, "We are not ignorant of the devil's devices." Be able to recognize his thoughts.

According to your faith, it will be done unto you. (Matthew 9:29)

Does this tell you how important faith is? A person cannot be saved without believing (faith) that Jesus paid the price for his sins and was raised from the dead. Let me simply explain to you about faith. It is a decision that one makes to believe or not to believe. It is up to each individual. If you believe that Jesus suffered the crucifixion of the cross for you and was raised from the dead, you are saved! You have become a child of God and are going to heaven when you die. John 3:36 says who believes in the Son (Jesus) has eternal life, but who rejects the son will not see life for God's wrath remains on them.

It is very simple. God the Father sent Jesus from heaven into the world to pay the price for the sins of the human race, and all who accept Jesus's sacrifice are forgiven of all their sins. That is so easy, and no one will have an excuse with God.

Let me warn all Christians of what Satan will do to you. He will bring up all the sinful things that you have done and try to get you to dwell on them to put you down, to destroy your righteousness that you received by faith in Jesus. Take your eyes off your past sins and put on the new man that God created when you believed in the Son of God.

Brother, I [Paul], count not myself to have apprehended, but this is one thing I do; forgetting those things which are behind, and reaching unto those things which are before [present]. (Philippians 3:13)

For by grace are you saved through *faith* [believing]; and not of yourselves, it is the gift of God: *not of works* less any man should boast [and say I earned by salvation]. (Ephesians 2:8–9, emphasis mine)

You are saved through faith and did not earn your salvation. Jesus Christ earned your salvation. You got forgiveness of your sins when you accepted what he did for you on the *cross*.

After you got saved and born again, you became a new person, and then you did "good works." Your good works came afterward, not before.

(The apostle Paul) And that you put on the *new man* which God has created in righteous and true holiness. (Ephesians 4:24, emphasis mine)

Can you imagine that God gave you a new spirit when you were born again that was created in righteousness and holiness and you are blameless of all past sins to him? Jesus Christ did it all—accepted the pain, the torment, and all the suffering. And we got credit for it just because of our faith in Christ.

What kind of "love" has God bestowed on us? Why did he do this? Because he (God) loved us! And God didn't stop there. He called us "sons" and "daughters"—we are his family. It brings tears to my eyes as I write this.

Pay attention to this Bible scripture:

In the body of His [Jesus] flesh through death to present you *Holy* and *unblameable* and *unreproveable* in His [God the Father] sight. (Colossians 1:22, emphasis mine)

This is what our faith in Jesus Christ's cross did for us to God the Father.

And you are *complete* in Him [Jesus] which is the Head of all principalities and power. (Colossians 2:10, emphasis mine)

Now, is there any question of where you stand with God the Father after reading the above two scriptures? Jesus did everything that needed to be done on the cross for our forgiveness of sin and to be born again. So many believers only know that the cross of Jesus was for the forgiveness of sin. They do not realize how important it was for Christ to be raised from the dead. If Christ was not raised from the dead, then we would have not been born again and become a new creature. Our salvation would not have been complete. If we were not changed, born again, we would have kept on sinning.

Pay attention to this scripture:

For if the dead rise not, then is not Christ raised?

And if Christ be not raised, your faith is vain and you are still in your sins. (1 Corinthians 15:16–17)

Is this scripture an eye-opener? By being changed, born again, we went from being unrighteous to righteous, from being unholy to holy. We became free from sin. Before our faith in Jesus, we were controlled by sin and the devil. Afterward, we were forgiven and free of being controlled by sin; we were a new person and had a new spirit with no sin in it because it was born (created) by the Word of God (Ezekiel 36:26).

Being born again, not of corruptible seed [the seed of man], but of the incorruptible seed *by the word* of God that liveth and abide forever. (Peter 1:23, emphasis mine)

Let us hear the conclusion of the whole matter [what God expects from us]: Fer God and keep his commandments, for this is the whole duty of man. (Ecclesiastes 12:13)

Fearing God is knowing who God is and who the devil is; and fear sinning, knowing the consequences of sin. God loves us. But one has to choose his ways, his commandments, and Jesus Christ.

God proved his love for us by sending Jesus Christ to earth to save us. But, if that was it, then we would have gone to heaven and just be people who were saved. But he didn't stop there. We became sons and daughters of the Most High God. We became his family!

Behold what manner of *love* the Father has given to us that we should be called Children of God. (1 John 3:1)

THE NAME OF JESUS CHRIST

There is another weapon that all Christians have been given to use to change things that exist in this world that we live in. That weapon is the "name of Jesus." However, like all things given to us from God, it must be received by faith. Christians must have faith in that name. The name of Jesus was the primary source of power that the disciples used.

God the Father gave that name all authority and power over everything that has a name. The only thing that is over the name itself is the Word of God. Everything is subordinate to the name of Jesus. Jesus has given us the right to use his name on the earth, but one has to have faith in that name to be effective. Here is an example of Peter using the name for healing:

> Now Peter and John went up together unto the temple at the hour of prayer. And a certain man lame from his mother's womb was carried whom they laid daily at the gate of the temple, which is called Beautiful, to ask alms [money] of them that entered into the temple. And Peter fastening his eyes upon him with John said: Look on us. Then Peter said, silver and gold have I none; but such as I have give I to you; In the name of Jesus Christ of Nazareth rise up and walk. And he [Peter] took him by the right hand and lifted him up and immediately his feet and ankle bones received strength. And all the people saw him walking and praising God. And when Peter saw it, he answered unto the people. You men of Israel, why marvel you at this? Or why look on you so earnestly on us as though by our own power or holiness we had made this man to walk? And his name through *faith in his name* has made this man strong. (Acts 3:1–2, 4, 6–7, 9, 12, 16)

Peter used the name of Jesus and had faith in the authority and power that God the Father gave this name, and Peter's spoken words in faith healed this lame man.

Everyone who accepted Jesus Christ's finished work on the cross and was born again has a right to use his name in this world. Remember God the Father is the One who gave authority and power in the name of Jesus; but you have to have faith in his name. This should be easy for Christians.

I have to add this: when you use this name for "good" and nothing happens at that moment, keep the faith and never let it go. God will do the rest at some point.

Jesus said: and whatsoever you shall ask in my name, that will I do, that the Father may be glorified in the Son. If you shall ask anything in my name, I [Jesus] will do it. (John 14:13–14)

Always use common sense when using this name or any other promises of God. God gave us a "sound mind" to use his power. His power is his Word. Let no Christian be caught not believing our Heavenly Father's Word. Be bold and use the name in your daily living.

CLOSING

It is imperative that you know whom you became after you were born again, a new creation. The Bible calls this "in Christ." Your new spirit was created in righteousness and holiness and blameless in the eyes of God. You must lock that in your mind. And when the devil attacks your mind and tells you that you are a sinner and you are evil and tries to belittle you mentally, you will know that is him and he is a liar. It is important that you recognize him and call him out and tell him you are saved, righteous, and committed to God and you resist him in the name of Jesus. This is spiritual maturity and pleasing unto God.

Once you are saved, all he (devil) wants to do is to make you unproductive in the body of Christ. God has "good works" for all of us to do while we are here on earth. As we mature in spiritual knowledge from the Word of God and increase in faith, God will reveal the good works he has planned for us to do while here on earth.

If any of you get diagnosed with cancer or any other serious disease, God's healing promises can save your life. He saved my life. God is no respecter of person and will heal any believer who has faith in his healing promises.

For unto us was the gospel [Word of God] preached as well as unto them; but the word preached *did not profit them* not being mixed with faith to them that heard it. (Hebrews 4:2)

Don't be a hearer only of the Word of God but a doer of the Word, which means do what the Word says. Confess and believe the healing promises. Do not be afraid, but do the teaching that I have told you and live. The promises are yes and Amen, so God has already said, "Yes! I will." Do not doubt and be ready to fight the good fight of faith in your mind. God loves you, and if you love him, then believe him and live.

If I asked you if you are holy, what would be your answer? Are you righteous? Are you blameless before God? Did you know that you are a new creation, a new person, a new creature, born again? Let us see what the Bible says about the above.

(The apostle Paul) And you put on the new man which after God is created in righteous and holiness. (Ephesians 4:24)

The new man Paul is referring to is the new person, born again, you became when you believed in Jesus Christ, the Son of God. And that person (you) is righteous and holy and blameless in God's eyes.

In the body of His [Jesus flesh through death present *you* holy and unblameable and unreproveable in His [God the Father] sight. (Colossians 1:22)

So you are righteous, holy, and blameless to God the Father.

All of what I have told you is what the Bible calls "in Christ." This is whom you became, in Christ.

You also became a son or daughter in the family of God. All this happened to you and for you because of Jesus Christ—willing to go to the cross for us! You are "complete" in him (Jesus), and there is nothing else that needs to be done. He did everything that was needed for us to be forgiven, born again, and reconciled to God the Father.

ABOUT THE AUTHOR

Ronald P. Braddock Sr. was saved when he was about twelve years old. He was also raised by a single mom. He and his brother, Jimmy, were poor. And they didn't know it for they always had enough food and clothes. Ronald decided at fifteen years old that he wanted to go to college, so he prayed this prayer: "Lord, I need to go to college, and the only way that this is possible is for me to get a scholarship in sports. I am good in baseball. I do not know if I am good enough, but if I am not, would you make me good enough?" After that prayer, he won every award one could win in high school in Savannah, Georgia. Ronald received a full scholarship to University of Georgia. God did not stop there. His junior year, he broke the highest batting record for a season by hitting 489 batting average. The record still holds after all these years! God is able to do more than we could ask or think according to the power that works in us (the Holy Spirit).